READ ALOUD • READ ALONE

Yea, Hooray! The Son Came Home Today!

And other **Bible Stories** about
WISDOM

By Christine Harder Tangvald
Illustrated by Ellen Joy Sasaki

Chariot Books™
David C. Cook Publishing Co

CONTENTS

Yea, Hooray! The Son Came Home Today! 3

The Wise Wise Men 13

King Solomon Said! 21

Let's Talk about It! 32

Chariot Books™ is an imprint of David C. Cook Publishing Co.
David C. Cook Publishing Co., Elgin, Illinois 60120
David C. Cook Publishing Co., Weston, Ontario
Nova Distribution Ltd., Newton Abbot, England

YEA, HOORAY! THE SON CAME HOME TODAY
© 1993 by Christine Harder Tangvald for text and Ellen Joy Sasaki for illustrations

All rights reserved. Except for brief excerpts for review purposes, no part of this book may be reproduced or used in any form without written permission from the publisher.
Designed by Elizabeth A. Thompson
First Printing, 1993
Printed in Singapore
97 96 95 94 93   5 4 3 2 1

Library of Congress Cataloging-in-Publication Data
Tangvald, Christine Harder
    Yea, hooray! the son came home today, and other Bible stories about wisdom/Christine Harder Tangvald; illustrated by Ellen Joy Sasaki.
    p. cm. — (Read aloud, read alone)
    Summary: Simple retellings of three Bible stories about the visit of the three Wise Men, the lesson of the Prodigal Son, and the wisdom of King Solomon.
    ISBN 0-7814-0927-6
    1. Wisdom—biblical teaching—juvenile literature. 2. Prodigal son (parable)—juvenile literature. 3. Magi—juvenile literature. 4. Solomon, King of Israel—juvenile literature. 5. Bible stories, English. [1. Bible stories. 2. Wisdom—biblical teaching. 3. Prodigal son (parable) 4. Magi. 5. Solomon, King of Israel.]
I. Sasaki, Ellen Joy, ill. II. Title. III. Series: Tangvald, Christine Harder, Read aloud, read alone.
BS680.W6T366 1993
220.9'505—dc20   93-9244
                                                                                      CIP
                                                                                       AC

All Scripture quotations in this publication are from the Holy Bible, New International Version. Copyright © 1973, 1978, 1984, International Bible Society. Used by permission of Zondervan Bible Publishers.

YEA, HOORAY!
THE SON CAME HOME TODAY!

WISDOM and Foolishness

"I AM LEAVING!" said the foolish foolish son to his father. "I don't like it here. Give me some money so I can go far, far away."

"Oh, please don't go," said the father. "I want you to stay. I want you to stay here with me."

"Give me my money NOW!"
said the foolish son.
"I am leaving!"
So the sad sad father gave his
foolish son some money.
The sad sad father watched
his son go far far away.

Walk, walk, walk went the foolish son.
WALK... WALK... WALK... WALK.

"This is GREAT,"

said the son.

"I like being by myself.

"What shall I do now? I know," said the son.

"I will use my money and have a party.

A BIG BIG party!"

And he did.

The foolish son used all his money
for big big parties.
"Oh, dear," said the foolish son.
"NOW WHAT WILL I DO?

"I don't have any
more money!
I spent it all.

"I am hungry.
I am cold.
And I am lonely.
WHAT WILL I DO?"

"I KNOW!" said the son. "I will get a job."

So the foolish son got a job.

He worked in a field of mud, taking care of pigs.

Squish, squish, squish

went the pigs in the mud.

OINK, OINK, OINK went the pigs in the mud.

Squish, squish, squish went the son in the mud.

"Oh, oh, oh!" said the son. "I do not like it here. I WANT TO GO HOME!"

"But will my father let me come home?"
asked the foolish foolish son.
"Maybe he doesn't WANT me anymore.
Maybe he doesn't LOVE me anymore.
Oh, dear. Oh, dear.
WHAT WILL I DO?"

"I know," thought the foolish son.
"I will ASK my father to FORGIVE me.
I will ask my father if I may come home."

Walk, walk, walk went the foolish son.
WALK... WALK...
WALK... WALK... WALK.

"Someone is coming," said the father.

"Who is it? Who can it be?

Why, it looks like my son.

It is my son! My son is coming home!

Yea! Yea! Hip-hip-hooray!" said the father.

"Oh, Father," said the son.

"I am so sorry. I was not wise.

I was foolish. May I please come home?

May I come home to stay?"

"Oh, yes," said the father.

"I WANT YOU HERE. I love you.

You may come home to stay.

Hey, everybody! My son is back.

My son is back home. Let's have a party!"

And they did.

You can find the son's story in your very own Bible. Ask a grown-up to read it with you. **Luke 15:11-24.**

THE WISE WISE MEN

A Story about **WISDOM**

"LOOK! LOOK!" said the first wise man.

"Look at the bright new star. See how it sparkles and shines!"

"WOW!" said the second wise man.

"Where did it come from? It is the brightest star in the sky."

"I have an idea," said the third wise man. "Let's follow the bright, new star. It will lead us to the new baby king."

"Oh, yes," said the first wise man.

"Let's do it. Let's follow the star right now."

And they did.

WALK, WALK, WALK. RIDE, RIDE, RIDE.

The wise men followed the bright new star.

WALK, WALK, WALK. RIDE, RIDE, RIDE.

"Where is the new baby king?" asked the wise wise men. "We have come to worship Him."

"WHAT?" yelled Herod, the horrid, very bad king. "There is another king in my land? WHERE IS HE?"

"We don't know," said the wise wise men. "We are following the bright, new star so we can find Him."

"Oh, yes," said Herod.

"You must find Him. Then come and tell me where He is. I want to worship Him, too."

But Herod, the horrid, very bad king,
did not want to worship the new baby king.
He wanted to kill the new baby king.
OH, NO! OH, DEAR!

"We will find Him," said the wise wise men.
"We will find the new baby king."

WALK, WALK, WALK. RIDE, RIDE, RIDE.
The bright, new star sparkled and shined brighter and brighter.
"HURRY, HURRY!" said the wise wise men.
"We are getting closer."

"HERE HE IS!" shouted the wise wise men.

"Yea! Yea! Hip-hip-hooray!"

It was JESUS.

Baby Jesus was the new baby king.

"Here are some presents we brought for You," said the wise wise men. "We hope You like them. They are the very best presents we have in all our land."

Then the wise wise men bowed down and worshiped baby Jesus.

They WORSHIPED God's own Son.

But those WISE WISE men did NOT tell Herod, the horrid, very bad king, where baby Jesus was.

"We are too WISE," they said. "We are too WISE to do that. We like baby Jesus. We love baby Jesus," said the WISE WISE men. "We will not tell Herod where Jesus is. Oh, no. We will just go home."

And they did.

You can find the wise men's story in your very own Bible. Ask a grown-up to read it with you. **Matthew 2:1-12.**

KING SOLOMON SAID!

A Story about **WISDOM**

King Solomon was WISE.
He was WISE, WISE, WISE.
God made King Solomon the wisest man
in all the land.
People came from far and near to ask King
Solomon questions.
They asked hard questions.
But King Solomon
knew the answers.
He knew because
God made him
WISE, WISE, WISE!

Some children asked King Solomon,

"Oh, wise King Solomon. What should we do? Some of our friends said, 'Come with us.

We are going to tease people.

We are going to do all kinds of BAD BAD things.' What should we do?"

KING SOLOMON SAID:

"Just tell them, 'NO! WE WON'T GO!'

Stay away from friends who get you into trouble.

Just tell them, 'NO! WE WON'T GO!'

And choose some new friends . . . *on the double!*"

"WE WILL," said the children. "WE WILL choose some new friends. Thank you, King Solomon. You are so WISE."

Proverbs 13:20

Once there was a big big family.

King Solomon came to their house for dinner.

"Come sit by US!" said all the boys.

"Come sit by US!" said all the girls.

"No! No! Over here," said all the boys.

"No! No! Over here," said all the girls.

"Sit by us!" "Sit by us!"

"Oh, King Solomon," cried the mother and father. "WHAT CAN WE DO?"

KING SOLOMON SAID:

"Stop! Stop! Oh, please, do not fight.

Do not be so loud at dinnertime.

This simply isn't right.

Let's be kind. Let's be nice.

Let's be gentle. Why not try it?

Let's eat the food that God gave us

in a little peace and quiet!"

"Oh, King Solomon, you are so WISE.

WE WILL TRY IT!"

And they all sat down and ate their food . . .

in wonderful peace and quiet!

Proverbs 17:1

One day, King Solomon saw some LAZY LAZY people.

"We are bored," said the lazy people.

"And we are hungry. Oh, wise King Solomon, what should we do?"

KING SOLOMON SAID:

"If you are hungry and want something to eat, you'd better get busy. Get up on your feet. Work like the ant. Look at all he can do. He works so hard and so should you!

"WORK! WORK! WORK!
That's the WISE thing to do.
You'll never be hungry.
Just try it . . . it's true!"

"Really?" asked all the people.
"Then we'd better get busy.
We'd better get to work!
Oh, thank you, King Solomon.
You are so WISE."

Proverbs 6:6

One day a big big crowd of people asked,
"King Solomon, we want to be happy.
What is the secret to a HAPPY HAPPY heart?"

KING SOLOMON SAID:

"Here are some ways to keep your heart glad.

Be kind and gentle, and try not to get mad.

Be very careful what words you use.

Be very careful which friends you choose.

"Be kind to your father.
Be kind to your mother.
Be kind to your sister.
Be kind to your brother.

"Be honest and truthful and do not pout!
Smile if you can from the inside . . . out!

"Just listen to God, trust His Word from the start.
And that is the secret to a HAPPY HAPPY heart!"

"Oh, King Solomon. You are so WISE!"

said all the people together.

Then they began to shout!

"HOORAY! HOORAY! HOORAY

for WISE KING SOLOMON!"

Proverbs 15:13

You can find King Solomon's story in your very own Bible. Ask a grown-up to read it with you. **I Kings 4:29-34.**

LET'S TALK ABOUT IT!

After you read the stories, talk about them with a grown-up.

> *For the Lord gives* **WISDOM**
> Proverbs 2:6a

- What did the foolish foolish son do that was **WISE**?
- What did the wise men do that was **WISE**?
- What are some things King Solomon said that were **WISE**?

WOW! Being **WISE** is more than being smart. What is a way you could be smart but not **WISE**? What is a way you could be smart and **WISE**?

Our Bible verse says God (the Lord) gives **WISDOM**. When do you need to ask God to make you **WISE**?

It makes God so happy when you obey His Word.
  Hooray for the foolish son who became **WISE**!
  Hooray for the wise men!
  Hooray for Solomon!
    . . . And Hooray for YOU!